AF454316

www.booksybee.com

FREE AUDIOBOOK

Get your ears ready for a treat!

Get your smartphone, scan the QR code and
enjoy the story, out loud!

Having trouble?
Email us at **info@booksybee.com**

First Published in 2023 by Booksy Bee
Based in Amsterdam, Netherlands
www.booksybee.com

ISBN: 978-90-833755-1-9

For any queries, please reach out to us
at **info@booksybee.com**

Hello Daycare

Mia's first day away from Mommy.

Written by
Rümeysa A. Hamid

Illustrated by
Orhan Ateş

Today is a special day! **Mia** is going to daycare for the first time.

Her **CUDDLY** bunny is coming too!

Mia's teacher, the sweet and friendly Miss **Lily**, greets her with a smile.

Despite Miss Lily's warmth, Mia still feels a bit sad because she knows her Mommy will be leaving soon.

"Don't worry, Mia", Mommy says, "I will stay with you for a little while".

"Shall we puzzle together? Or would you like to do some colouring?" asks Mommy.

It's time to say goodbye but Mia finds
it very difficult.

With all those new faces around, everything feels
a little strange.

Mommy bends down and says, "I understand, sweetheart. It's perfectly normal to feel nervous because you have just met your teacher and these other children".

"As soon as you get to know them you will really like it here.
And remember that Mommy always comes back".

All the kids sit around the table for breakfast. Mia's tears have dried, but she is still feeling sad.

Miss Lily
asks everyone
what toppings they want
on their sandwich. Mia chooses a
delicious jam sandwich. Time to feast!

After breakfast, they form a circle. Miss Lily reads a book about adorable baby animals.

It's outdoor play time!
All the kids run outside.

Mia swiftly swooshes down the slide and her giggles fill the air.

Then she goes cycling with other children.
Mia has already made so many new friends!

With every passing moment,
Mia starts to like the daycare more and more.

Everyone had so much fun playing outside and now it's time for a nap.
Miss Lily gently tucks Mia into her comfy bed.

But Mia has trouble falling asleep because she misses her Mommy. Thankfully, she has her bunny to cuddle with. They wizz off to dreamland together.

Mia is **awake**, feeling refreshed and ready for more adventures. She is now going to play with the blocks.

"Wow! Look!" Mia exclaims.
"I built such a tall tower!"

Guess who is waiting at the door.
It's Mia's Mommy!
Mia rushes over to her.

They give each other
a big **BEAR HUG**.

Mia is happy that
Mommy is back!

You see little one!
Mommy always comes
back.

Now it's time to go home...

BooksyBee

9 789083 375519